Outdoor Farm, Indoor Farm

Outdoor Farm.

LINDSAY H. METCALF

Indoor Farm

Illustrated by XIN LI

ASTRA YOUNG READERS

AN IMPRINT OF ASTRA BOOKS FOR YOUNG READERS

New York

Outdoors, indoors,
big or bitty,
through the seasons,
country, city . . .

DEAR EFREM,
THANK YOU FOR
VISITING US. HERE
IS OUR NEW DRONE.

I NAMED IT BOB.

Farms are farms no matter where.
What's the recipe they share?

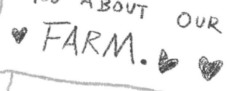

DEAR EMMA,

IT WAS SO FUN TO VISIT YOUR FARM. MOM'S LETTING ME WORK AS A RESEARCH ASSISTANT AT OUR FARM.

WOULD YOU SHARE MORE ABOUT BOB?

I WOULD LOVE TO TELL YOU ABOUT OUR

♥ FARM. ♥ ♥

Sprinkle in *spring* . . .
Outdoor farm,
field meets sky.

Indoor farm,
trays stack high.

Outdoor farm,
tractors toil.

Indoor farm,
zero soil.

Outdoor farm,
sunlight beams.

Indoor farm,
color streams.

Simmer in *summer* . . .
Outdoor farm,
spritz the shoots.

Indoor farm,
mist the roots.

Outdoor farm,
map the field.

Indoor farm,
track the yield.

Outdoor farm,
weed control.

Indoor farm,
sky patrol.

Slice through *fall* . . .

Outdoor farm, combines clip.

Indoor farm,
scissors snip.

Outdoor farm,
hit the scale.

Indoor farm,
prep for sale.

Outdoor farm,
crank and pour!

Indoor farm,
steer to store.

Savor in *winter* . . .

Outdoor farm,
growing slows.
Mend machines
while fire glows.

Indoor farm
hums along.
Fine-tune climate.
Green stays strong.

The recipe for farm-fresh flavor:
sprinkle, simmer, slice, and savor.

Grains to greens,
country, city,
outdoors, indoors,
big or bitty . . .

DEAR EMMA,

MY FRIENDS AT SCHOOL
ENJOYED SEEING
YOUR DRONE, BOB.
THEY WERE ALSO CURIOUS
ABOUT YOUR TRACTOR.
DOES THAT HAVE A
NAME TOO?

Season crops with innovation—
science plus determination.

Why Farms Are Changing

The world population is expected to grow to 9.7 billion by 2050. That's about two billion more mouths to feed than in 2023, when this sentence was written. To help us all survive, farmers will have to produce about 70 percent more food, according to the United Nations.

We can't simply clear more land to grow more crops. Doing so removes animal habitats. It reduces biodiversity, or the variety of living things, such as plants and animals. Clearing land also takes away trees that gulp carbon dioxide from the air. Our atmosphere has too much carbon dioxide produced by human activity, especially from burning fossil fuels like coal and petroleum and even from the process of growing food. Carbon dioxide and similar gases trap heat from the sun and warm Earth's temperature, causing climate change. Because outside conditions are changing, Earth is experiencing more destructive storms, longer drought periods, and more intense heat. Simply put: climate change hurts all life on Earth—including the plants we eat.

Farms must become more efficient to combat changing conditions. This means farms not only must be ready for changing weather patterns, but also must incorporate technology and creative thinking to grow *more* food on the *same* amount of land using *fewer* resources. And farmers must do all that while reducing their own climate footprint—the measure of carbon they release into the atmosphere.

Outdoor Farms

Outdoor farms take advantage of natural sunlight, soil, and open air. They can spread across land the size of several thousand football fields or tuck into small backyards. Outdoor farms vary greatly depending on the local climate and soil type. Sunlight is free, so some outdoor farms have solar panels to generate renewable electricity with no carbon emissions. Outdoor farmers are also devising ways to conserve irrigation water, protect soil health, and map weak growth spots using drones or satellites. They are saving resources by targeting weed control, fertilization, and pest control efforts on limited areas.

Indoor Farms

Indoor farms are a small but growing portion of the world's food producers taking root where open land is scarce. Small indoor farms can be found in cities, schools, and even on the International Space Station. Some indoor farms fill large warehouses with racks or towers of plants grown with aeroponics (a nutrient solution is misted onto bare roots), hydroponics (plants grow in water enriched with nutrients), or sometimes aquaponics (hydroponics plus fish, where fish poop is fertilizer!). Indoor farms can be greenhouses bathed in sunlight, or enclosed buildings that must use electric lights. In this book, the indoor farm uses the technology of aeroponics, but most indoor farms use hydroponics.

Planting

Tractors pull planters that sow seeds or seedlings at just the right depth and spacing. Some planters can be programmed to change the seeding rate, automatically planting fewer seeds in areas that previously produced lower yields—the amount of food harvested. Instead of ploughing dead plants under the soil, many farmers now plant seeds directly among decomposing plants. This no-till farming protects the soil's microscopic organisms, which break down the dead plants. New plants' roots pull nutrients from fertile soil formed from broken-down, decomposed plants. This encourages stronger new growth that bears more food on the same amount of land.

Planting

In indoor farms, seeds grow without soil—sometimes on cloth—undisturbed by bad weather or changing seasons. Large vertical farms fit into relatively small spaces by rising up instead of out—sometimes as high as a telephone pole (36 feet)! Not all types of crops make sense to plant indoors—yet. The field of indoor farming, especially vertical farming, is still new, and growers are looking for ways to lower expenses before they plant a wider variety of crops. Growers can earn more money from plants that produce a lot of food in a small area, using shallow root systems. For now, that means planting mostly salad greens and herbs. Bushy plants such as squash and tall plants such as corn take too much room.

Growing

Farmers must feed plants with fertilizer from either natural or man-made sources. To find out which nutrients the soil needs, farmers can have soil samples tested in a lab. Then global positioning systems (GPS) can tell tractors where to fertilize, and how much. Many farms must also water growing plants through irrigation. Sensors help some irrigation systems add the right amount at the right time. Some newer devices zap crop-damaging weeds with electricity or lasers. To make outdoor farming jobs more efficient and eco-friendly, some companies are building powerful, electric tractors that don't need drivers at all!

Harvesting

Some outdoor crops, such as lettuce, must be harvested by hand. Other outdoor crops, such as grains, are harvested once a year with a combine. This machine cuts the plant, separates the food from its casing, and throws out the parts that can't be eaten. Newer combines can be as tall as a small house! Once a crop ripens, it's a race against time to harvest the plants before they spoil or weather destroys them. Some combine operators save time by driving and cutting while unloading their crop into a moving cart. On grain farms, truck drivers transport grain to a big storage area called an elevator.

Growing

A plant needs structural support, water, nutrients, and air—but not soil. Scientists can boost growth and flavor by experimenting with a plant's recipe of nutrients, lighting, temperature, and more. Indoor farms often use low-energy LED lighting and split the light spectrum into colors, using only the ones found to be most beneficial for growing, such as red and blue light. Indoor farms also use little water compared with outdoor farms. Both the water and air of indoor farms are filtered in an effort to keep insects and germs out. Machines and robots sometimes aid in the care of the plants growing indoors.

Harvesting

With perfect temperature, light, and nutrition, the planting-to-harvest cycle happens faster than it does outdoors and can be repeated many times year-round. At some indoor farms, workers wearing gloves, hairnets, and clean uniforms clip plants at harvest time by hand. At others, conveyor belts send whole trays of plants through harvest machines, which cut many greens automatically. Crops grown with few or no germs or pesticides do not need to be washed for the consumer, saving water. Large indoor farms can produce more than a million pounds of leafy greens each year.

Activities

Farmers 2050: Sustainable outdoor farming role-playing game. farmers2050.com

Hydroponics Farm in a Bottle: Build your own hydroponics farm at home or in the classroom using a plastic bottle. lindsayhmetcalf.com

Purple Plow: Agriscience challenges for students and classrooms. purpleplow.org

Videos

"Vertical Farming," by Reactions Everyday Chemistry: youtube.com/watch?time_continue=0&v=rEw-VfFkUik

Virtual tour of BrightFarms hydroponic farm: vimeo.com/410603232

Selected Sources

AeroFarms vertical farming company: aerofarms.com

Food and Agriculture Organization of the United Nations: fao.org

NASA Climate Kids: climatekids.nasa.gov/climate-change-meaning/

National Agriculture in the Classroom: agclassroom.org

A combine harvester dumps wheat into a grain cart pulled by a tractor.
Photo by Patrick Pleul/AP Images

A worker wears a sterile suit, gloves, and booties to check plants at a vertical farm.
Photo by Alexandr Kryazhev/Sputnik via AP

For all the farm kids, especially Haddie, Brynna,
and Callie —*LHM*
For all the kids who are curious about where their food
comes from —*XL*

Astra Young Readers, an imprint of Astra Books for Young Readers,
a division of Astra Publishing House
astrapublishinghouse.com

Printed in China

Acknowledgment

The publisher thanks Paul P. Gauthier, PhD, of the University of
Queensland, Australia, for his careful review of the text and
illustrations.

ISBN: 978-1-63592-591-3 (hc)
ISBN: 978-1-63592-592-0 (eBook)
Library of Congress Control Number: 2021925699

First edition

10 9 8 7 6 5 4 3 2 1

Design by Barbara Grzeslo
The text is set in Neutraface Demi.
The illustrations are done digitally
in Photoshop.